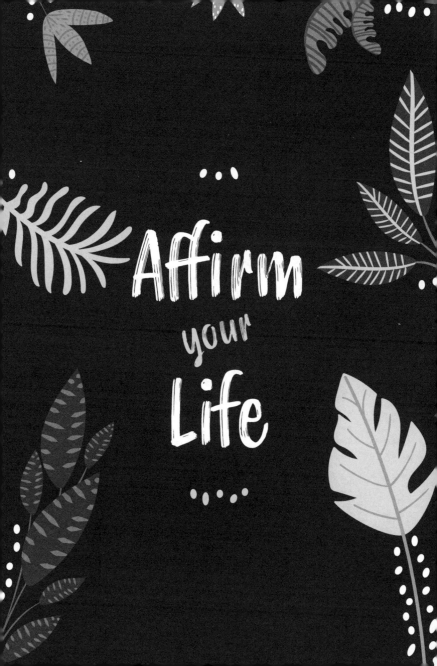

# Affirm
## *your*
# Life

Your
*Affirmations*
**JOURNAL**
for *Purpose* and
Personal
*Effectiveness*

Becca Anderson
Inspired by the Wisdom of Stephen R. Covey

CORAL GABLES

Curated and edited by Annie Oswald, Natasha Vera, and Diana Laura Valcárcel
Published by Mango Publishing Group, a division of Mango Media Inc.

Cover Design, Layout & Design: Morgane Leoni
Illustrations: © Snejana Sityaeva & © Nadezda Grapes

For permission requests, please contact the publisher at:
Mango Publishing Group
2850 S Douglas Road, 2nd Floor
Coral Gables, FL 33134 USA
info@mango.bz

For special orders, quantity sales, course adoptions and corporate sales, please email the publisher at sales@mango.bz. For trade and wholesale sales, please contact Ingram Publisher Services at customer.service@ingramcontent.com or +1.800.509.4887.

Affirm Your Life: Your Affirmations Journalfor Purpose and Personal Effectiveness

Library of Congress Cataloging-in-Publication number: 2020940927
ISBN: (print) 978-1-64250-265-7, (ebook) 978-1-64250-266-4
BISAC category code GAM021000—GAMES & ACTIVITIES / Guided Journals

Printed in the United States of America

"I affirm to you the tremendous potential you have, not beyond anything you could ever imagine."

—Stephen R. Covey

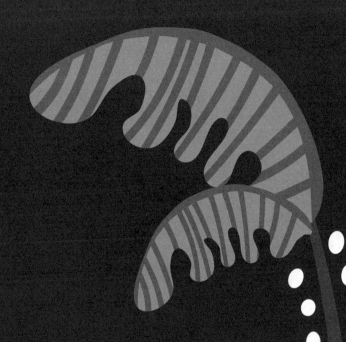

"Affirmations are our mental vitamins,
providing the supplementary positive
thoughts we need to balance the
barrage of negative events and thoughts
we experience daily."

—Peggi Spears and Tia Walker,
  The Inspired Caregiver

# Contents

Introduction | The Win Before You Begin ............ 8

Chapter 1 | Choose Your Power ............ 16

Chapter 2 | Create Your Future ............ 40

Chapter 3 | Make "It" Happen ............ 62

Chapter 4 | Think: Abundance ............ 80

Chapter 5 | Learn Soul Language ............ 100

Chapter 6 | No Root Grows Alone ............ 118

Chapter 7 | Make Renewal a Habit ............ 130

Conclusion | Affirm Your Life Now ............ 150

Sources ............ 160

About the Author ............ 161

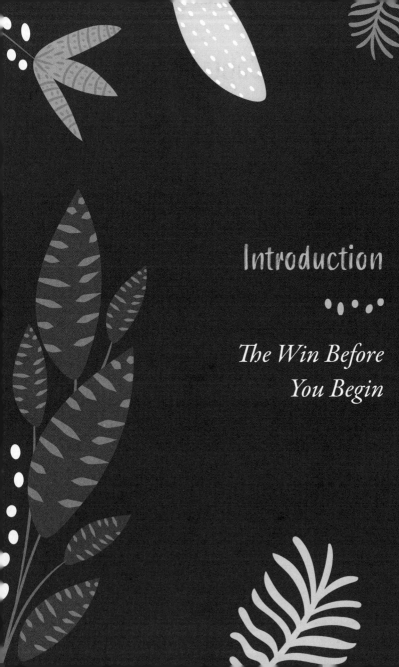

# Introduction

••••

*The Win Before
You Begin*

Once upon a time, in the bell bottom-clad days of the late '70s, there was a gentleman who developed a set of habits on how to live a more fulfilling life, a more *effective* life. One in which you took responsibility for your own circumstances, relationships, and took proactive steps in changing them for the better. And he kept things pretty simple, too. This set of habits didn't go on and on forever—no, there are only *seven* of them.

These habits I'm referring to are, of course, what are known today as The 7 Habits.

The 7 Habits are timeless. Even if you weren't around when the late Stephen R. Covey penned his famous book, which has since become a powerful guide in self-transformation for millions of people, you probably have at least heard of *The 7 Habits of Highly Effective People* and its impact.

The application of these habits can help anyone, at any time in history, and at whatever point you are at in your life. And together they accomplish one specific thing: they give you a strong foundation from which to lead a successful and fulfilling life. When you have developed a strong internal core—one based on values and being proactive—you are much better equipped to deal with events when they inevitably "hit the fan" and come out stronger than before. It's that simple.

But learning and living the habits isn't just for personal benefit—the effects will ripple out into all the aspects of your life. Your work life, personal life, and spiritual life. The habits are based upon *universal* and *timeless* principles of effectiveness. That's simply what they do when you introduce them into your life and make them, well, *habits*.

The effect these habits have had on people's lives has been tremendous and inspiring. But what Stephen R. Covey didn't know when he wrote the book, however, was that it was only the beginning. (Or maybe he did after all, and was eerily omniscient that way.) The 7 Habits have permeated all aspects of our culture, specifically when it comes to proactivity. To explain what I mean, I'll tell you about a recent conversation I had with my cousin, Tanya.

One day, Tanya called me out of the blue imploring me to drive her to Yosemite National Park, which is only a few hours away from our hometown of San Francisco. Rock climbing is a big hobby of hers, so I wasn't surprised. However, she had recently sprained her ankle while rock climbing in the same park a few weeks before. For several days after she got her cast on, she was quite gloomy and restless. When we got in the car, I asked her what I had been wondering about ever since she called me. Why did she want to go when she clearly couldn't climb for another few weeks?

"To keep training, of course," was her answer.

I was dumbstruck, but I decided to let it slide. I was used to Tanya's devil-may-care attitude and slightly amused to see how this would turn out. (She hadn't even brought her tools.) When we got there, she hobbled on her crutches over to the tall, jagged rock she was attempting to master before she was injured. Once she got to a good vantage point, she plopped down, staring up at the rock's face. Actually, she wasn't really staring up— more like staring *down* at it, defiantly.

I walked over to join her, glad I brought a book for company. After several minutes of her standing completely still, however, I huffed and closed my book.

"What in the world are you doing?" I asked.

"*Training*, like I told you," she replied as if it were obvious.

"I don't get it," I scoffed. "You can't climb yet, so what's the deal?"

"Next time I do, I'm going to get all the way to the top. As I'm looking at it now, I can see what route I should have taken. You see that little crevice there?" She pointed at some nondescript spot on the massive rock. I squinted. "That's where I *should* have put my foot." She said, looking down at her bulky, plaster-wrapped leg. "I decided that even though I can't climb *now*, that doesn't mean I can't get better. I've basically already gotten to the top in my mind right now," she chuckled.

I sat there for several moments, not knowing what to say. I was surprised. She was totally right. As the saying goes, the battle is won before it even begins.

While I was sitting cluelessly with my book, Tanya now knew several better routes to take on her next climb. Instead of sulking back at home, she had chosen to not be a victim. She had chosen to take the steps that she knew were in her power, instead of feeling powerless.

It had been many years since I read *The 7 Habits*, but my mind somehow told me that she was being *proactive*. The very first habit.

When I questioned her about it, she said she hadn't read the book at all. However, both of her parents had, and had seemed to drill several of its key lessons into the both of us. One was the power to choose how you react. To choose how powerful you are in a situation. You see, Tanya had interpreted this first habit in her own way, without even realizing it!

When I gave it some thought, I realized there were several ways that I was (also unknowingly!) applying principles of being proactive and "not

a victim" in my life. And I'll bet that you do as well, reader. That's what this guided journal aims to do—to introduce (or re-introduce) you to the Habits in a whole new way.

Using the timeless wisdom of Dr. Covey, this journal gently guides you through The 7 Habits with the intention of empowering you. I wrote about these habits in a newer, perhaps slightly odd way. But that is because, once learned, each person always makes them uniquely their own. The principles are there simply to lead you.

With confidence-boosting affirmations and journaling to open your mind and help you explore means of improvement, *Affirm Your Life* is the perfect tool if you are seeking to make lasting changes in your life. But tools are only effective if you put them to use. Each day, as you journal your thoughts into discovery, pick an affirmation for the day and keep it in your mind. Then, get inspired by the wise words of the many pioneers, entrepreneurs, artists, and great thinkers in this book.

The Habits and guidance in this book will aid you in re-centering your life's motivation, goals, priorities, relationships, peace of mind, and more. As I mentioned—and Dr. Covey probably intended—it's only the beginning. Though I started this book with a "once upon a time" story, the tale hasn't ended yet. On the contrary, it continues with you.

It's time to affirm your life.

—BECCA ANDERSON

## Habit 1
### Be Proactive
Take responsibility for your life. You are not a victim of genetics, circumstance, or upbringing. Live life from your Circle of Influence.

## Habit 2
### Begin with the End in Mind
Define your values, mission, and goals in life. Live life based upon your vision of your life.

## Habit 3
### Put First Things First
Prioritize your activities and focus on what matters most. Spend more of your time in Quadrant II: the quadrant of important but not urgent.

## Habit 4
### Think Win-Win
Have an everyone-can-win attitude; be happy for the success of others.

## Habit 5
### Seek First to Understand, Then to be Understood
Listen to people empathically and then ask to be heard.

## Habit 6
### Synergize
Value and celebrate differences so that you can achieve more than you ever could have alone.

## Habit 7
### Sharpen the Saw
Consistently recharge your batteries in all four dimensions: physical, mental, spiritual, and social/emotional.

# Chapter 1

• • • •

*Choose Your Power*

"EACH OF US GUARDS A GATE OF CHANGE THAT CAN BE OPENED ONLY FROM THE INSIDE."

—Stephen R. Covey

# Introducing You to Your Potential

Anyone who has tried to make a situation better by doing what they *can*, instead of focusing on what they can't do, has unknowingly embraced the first Habit to becoming an effective person: "Be Proactive." It has become part of the culture of positive thinking.

I recently met up with my old friend Jessica, not yet thirty years old, who graduated college with an excellent degree, tremendous talent, and lots of energy. As we caught up and began talking about our professional lives over two warm lattes, she expressed to me how frustrated she felt in her work life—lost and slightly unmotivated. This was odd for Jessica, as she has always been such an upbeat person. She assured me she liked her career, but just felt helpless in growing her dream of making a huge impact in that company and moving up. So, I asked her a few questions.

"Well, what is your company's highest priority right now?"

She couldn't say. She wrapped her hands around her coffee cup, deep in thought.

> "THE MOST COMMON WAY PEOPLE GIVE UP THEIR POWER IS BY THINKING THEY DON'T HAVE ANY."
>
> —Alice Walker, American author

"When was the last time you met one-on-one with your manager to talk about how you could help achieve the company's goals?"

Jessica said she hadn't met with her manager one-on-one since she was hired, three years before.

Finally I asked her, "What have you personally contributed to the company?"

She thought for a moment and quietly answered: "I've probably saved the company half a million dollars in the last year."

"Um...who knows that besides you?" I asked her, slightly in awe.

"I make out a report once a week for my boss...but I don't think he reads it. And sometimes I'm so busy and burdened with trivial tasks that I never get the chance to bring it up."

My dear friend looked crestfallen. I felt deeply for her—her energy was being drained, her excitement was gone, her dreams of making a great impact on the company and world had shrunken down to fulfilling a mere job description. She had allowed herself to be reduced to a "job description with legs." Her wins weren't celebrated because somewhere along the way, she stopped thinking they were worthy enough.

Some of the blame for her situation probably had to do with poor company management, but her descent probably happened slowly, without her ever realizing it. She had lost track of her own worth.

At the core, there is one simple, overarching reason why so many people remain unsatisfied in their jobs, relationships, and life. Personal dissatisfaction stems from an incomplete paradigm of who they are

and what they can become. *They have a fundamentally flawed view of themselves.*

You cannot find your value as a human being outside of yourself—it comes from inside. Deep down, you must know that you are a being of virtually infinite potential, and, unlike a machine, you have the power to choose what you will be. Too many of us base our self-worth on externals, on being compared to other people. So many people equate their self-worth—or the worth of what they achieve—to what it looks like on the outside. Riches, a seemingly successful career, a picture-perfect home, a [insert adjective] body, etc. You are as worthy and powerful as you choose to be. No one can truly stop you, except yourself.

Just like my cousin Tanya chose to not be a victim, eventually so did Jessica. Being proactive is the essence of the first habit. The first stone that causes the ripple-effect of positive change.

> "FREEING YOURSELF WAS ONE THING, CLAIMING OWNERSHIP OF THAT FREED SELF WAS ANOTHER."
>
> —**Toni Morrison**, *Beloved*

# Repeat After Me

## AFFIRMATIONS TO BOOST YOUR CONFIDENCE

You are more powerful than you can imagine. But only *you* can determine *how* powerful. Each day, read one of these affirmations and keep it in your mind throughout the whole day. That way, when you face a challenge, whether external or internal, you will be reminded that you have the choice in how to act.

"WE ONLY WANT THAT WHICH IS GIVEN NATURALLY TO ALL PEOPLE OF THE WORLD, TO BE MASTERS OF OUR OWN FATE, ONLY OF OUR FATE, NOT OF OTHERS, AND IN COOPERATION AND FRIENDSHIP."

—Golda Meir, former prime minister of Israel

"IN THE WORLD THROUGH WHICH I TRAVEL, I AM ENDLESSLY CREATING MYSELF."

—Frantz Fanon, French West Indian philosopher

I have the power to make change happen.

I offer the world something that is unique and needed.

My strengths are leading me on a path to success.

My contribution will make a difference in my career and the world.

I am energized by my work and my passions.

I have powerful ideas.

I productively work with the same enthusiasm that I started a the project with.

Today, I abandon my old habits and take up new, more positive ones.

My choices lead to a positive outcome for myself and others.

# Explore through Journaling

"IF WE DON'T CHANGE, WE DON'T GROW. IF WE DON'T GROW, WE AREN'T REALLY LIVING."

—Gail Sheehy, American author

"BEING PROACTIVE IS A PILLAR OF SPIRITUAL GROWTH AND MEANINGFUL DEVELOPMENT."

—Eli Landa, Norwegian model

"IT WILL NEVER RAIN ROSES: WHEN WE WANT TO HAVE MORE ROSES, WE MUST PLANT MORE ROSES."

—George Eliot (Mary Anne Evans), English writer

"A GENIUS IS THE ONE MOST LIKE HIMSELF."

—Thelonious Monk, American jazz musician

Are you about to take a big leap forward? Make a big decision? Start a new project? Write down your purpose and motivation behind it. That way, if you feel yourself slipping midway, you can revisit this page to remind you why yourself started.

What is one setback you have faced recently? Explore how you could claim your power and take action in a different way.

_____

_____

_____

_____

_____

_____

_____

_____

_____

_____

_____

_____

_____

_____

_____

_____

_____

_____

Explore some of the ways you could lose momentum in an upcoming endeavor, and how you would overcome those barriers if they occurred.

When do you feel most confident? Where are you? Around which people? When was the last time you felt brave and fearless? Brainstorm how you could tap into those feelings more frequently.

Now consider the situations that fill you with hesitation and doubt. When does this happen? How can you avoid or turn these situations around in the future?

_____

_____

_____

_____

_____

_____

_____

_____

_____

_____

_____

_____

_____

_____

_____

_____

Think about the people you spend the majority of your time with and list them here. Do these people influence you in a positive or negative way? Do these people encourage you to become the best version of yourself? If yes, how so? If no, why not?

_____

_____

_____

_____

_____

_____

_____

_____

_____

_____

_____

_____

_____

_____

_____

_____

_____

Identify and list some characteristics about yourself that you think are preventing you from having a powerful, proactive day. After you have listed these traits, select one and write how you can change it. Try implementing these changes over the next week. After the week has ended, write down your results. Did you have success in trying to change this trait? Yes or no? Explain. Continue doing this for each trait!

_____

_____

_____

_____

_____

_____

_____

_____

_____

_____

_____

_____

_____

_____

_____

_____

_____

Have you ever had the desire to make an impact in a certain field or for a particular cause? What is the smallest first step you can take to make it happen? What about after that?

What does the phrase "being a victim" mean to you? Can you think of some ways this might happen, and how you would take back your power?

_____

_____

_____

_____

_____

_____

_____

_____

_____

_____

_____

_____

_____

_____

_____

_____

_____

_____

"Sometimes it is the people no one can imagine anything of who do the things no one can imagine."

—Alan Turing, English mathematician

# The Ifs and Wills

There are certain things we have control over, and others that are simply out of our reach. (In other words, you can relax about not being able to control your country's economy. But you can definitely do something about your own income!) It's important to be realistic about each. Check how you talk to yourself about the things in your life! Here is one way to determine which category each of your concerns falls into.

| If | Will |
|---|---|
| "I would be less stressed **if** I had my house paid off." | "I **will** start a side hustle so I can pay off my mortgage faster." |
| "**If** only I had a partner who was a better listener." | "I **will** start communicating more effectively and listening to my partner." |
| "**If** only I had my degree already." | "I **will** enroll in one class next semester." |

Now try a few of your own recurring "if" thoughts, and see if you can turn them around in the "will" column.

| If | Will |
|---|---|
|  |  |
|  |  |
|  |  |
|  |  |

# Chapter 2

*Create Your Future*

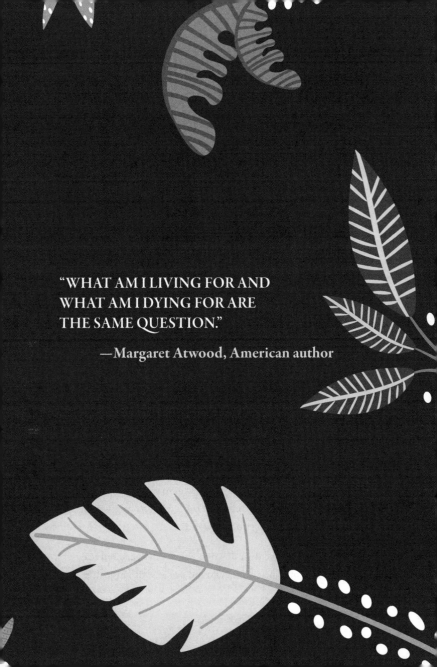

"WHAT AM I LIVING FOR AND
WHAT AM I DYING FOR ARE
THE SAME QUESTION."

—Margaret Atwood, American author

# Discover Your End in Mind

The second Habit, "Begin with the End in Mind," means picturing where you want to end up in your life. It means deciding what you ultimately value and then setting goals based on that. This could work on a smaller scale—what you want to get out of today—or a lifetime scale. It's kind of like asking yourself, "How exactly can I get *there*?"

> **"THE ONLY THING WORSE THAN BEING BLIND IS HAVING SIGHT BUT NO VISION."**
>
> **—Helen Keller, American activist**

At an early point in his career, the young author Charles Dickens was discouraged. He had a wife and four children to support and another child on the way. He was also essentially out of a job. Plagued by self-doubt and mounting financial pressures, he found it hard to write. Instead, he spent long, sleepless nights walking the streets of London.

He loved talking to strangers. As he talked by night with those struggling and living in the street, observing firsthand the social strains of child labor, poverty, and hopelessness, an idea formed in his mind. These sights fueled his passion to help the poor, and he began to see beyond his own problems. How could he make a difference? What did he have within himself to contribute to making a better world?

On October 14, 1843, Dickens sat down to write with a renewed zeal. He felt purpose. He combined this newfound passion with his native strength as a writer to create a small book that he hoped would change the world, as well as his own fortune. Six weeks later, he published *A Christmas Carol*, an immortal story that at once became wildly popular and transformed public opinion. Some observers connect the beginning of Britain's social reform movement with the publication of the book.

For Dickens, it was also the beginning of a prosperous writing career. His novels made him wealthy, enabling him to get involved in educating and re-integrating the poor into society through his Urania Cottage charity.

What was it that re-charged Dickens and re-focused his great career? Lonely nights hearing the stories of the poor, he at last found his mission. He found that this unique combination of natural talent, passion for a cause, and the call of his conscience could fill a great need in the world. He found his "End in Mind."

A really helpful exercise to help you discover what Dickens eventually did (and in as little time as possible) is to craft a "mission statement" for your life. We are always centered in the middle of chaos. It never goes away. Your mission statement sums up the best you have to offer to the challenges that excite you. With your mission statement in hand, you have the direction for your life goals.

> "IT'S IMPORTANT TO FIND YOUR INNER PEACE. FOR ME, IT'S LITERALLY LOOKING AT THE BIGGER PICTURE. WHEN I THINK ABOUT THE SIZE OF THE UNIVERSE, I FEEL LIKE ANY PROBLEMS I'M SURROUNDED BY ARE SO SMALL. I JUST DO MY BEST TO REACT TO CHAOS WITH LOVE, AND HOPEFULLY, OTHER PEOPLE WILL CATCH ON AND DO THINGS OUT OF LOVE, TOO."
>
> **—Melanie Iglesias, American actress**

# Repeat After Me

## AFFIRMATIONS FOR
## YOUR "END IN MIND"

Affirmations are often overlooked as a source of focus. Try saying one of these (or all!) aloud each day this week in order to remind you of the path you've paved to the bright future ahead of you.

"THE FUTURE BELONGS TO THOSE WHO
BELIEVE IN THE BEAUTY OF THEIR DREAMS."

—Eleanor Roosevelt, American activist and first lady

"HE WHO HAS A WHY TO LIVE FOR
CAN BEAR ALMOST ANY HOW."

—Friedrich Nietzsche, "Twilight of the Idols, or,
How to philosophize with a hammer"

"YESTERDAY IS GONE. TOMORROW HAS NOT YET
COME. WE HAVE ONLY TODAY. LET US BEGIN."

—Mother Teresa, Indian missionary

I know what my values are and I live a life based upon them.

I have consciously chosen my own future.

I move forward eagerly with a clear vision of where I want to be and where I want to go.

I feel at peace with myself because I know where I'm going.

I have set reasonable and achievable goals and I will achieve, and even surpass, them.

I am not a victim of the past.

I envision a bright future ahead of me and I make daily progress toward that future.

I live a principle-centered life and things and opinions cannot deter me.

When I face a crossroads of life I have already made the decision which way to go.

# Craft Your Mission

## JOURNALING FOR YOUR "END IN MIND"

*"YOU ARE INFLUENCED BY YOUR GENES, BY YOUR
UPBRINGING, AND BY YOUR ENVIRONMENT,
BUT YOU ARE NOT DETERMINED BY THEM."*

—Stephen R. Covey

It's a rainy day and you're stuck indoors. You decide to put on some music and do a jigsaw puzzle. You pour out all 1,000 pieces, spreading them out across the large table. You check out the lid of the box to see what you're putting together. But there's no picture—it's blank. How will you ever be able to finish the puzzle without knowing what it looks like? What a difference a mere photo would make! Without it, you have no clue where to start.

Now think about your own life. How do you picture it?

*"THAT IS HAPPINESS; TO BE DISSOLVED INTO
SOMETHING COMPLETE AND GREAT."*

—Willa Cather, *My Ántonia*

Do you have an end in mind? What is your mission statement?

Do you have a clear picture of who you want to be one year from now?

_____

_____

_____

_____

_____

_____

_____

_____

_____

Five years from now?

_____

_____

_____

_____

_____

_____

_____

_____

Twenty years from now?

_____

_____

_____

_____

_____

_____

_____

_____

_____

_____

_____

_____

_____

_____

_____

_____

_____

_____

_____

_____

Everyone has a unique gift—often we have several. It seems to be a natural principle. So what comes naturally to you? Think about it.

What do you do easily and well? If someone were to ask your friends or coworkers to list your talents, what would they say?

_____

_____

_____

_____

_____

_____

_____

_____

_____

_____

_____

_____

_____

_____

_____

_____

What do people ask you to do because you're good at it? (Whether you like it or not.)

Somewhere within you is a simmering pot of excitement that needs an outlet. Here are some questions to think about that will lead you to a better understanding of your passions.

What do you spend your free time on?

_____

_____

_____

_____

_____

_____

_____

_____

_____

_____

_____

_____

_____

_____

_____

_____

_____

What do you get energized about? What do you feel like arguing about?

_____

_____

_____

_____

_____

_____

_____

_____

What do you read?

_____

_____

_____

_____

_____

_____

_____

_____

What did you do as a child that intrigued you?

_____

_____

_____

_____

_____

_____

_____

_____

What Dickens-like experiences have you had that have excited you?

_____

_____

_____

_____

_____

_____

_____

_____

_____

If you could spend one hour with any person who ever lived, who would that be? Why that person? What would you ask them?

"What you know today can affect what you do tomorrow. But what you know today cannot affect what you did yesterday."

—Zora Neale Hurston, American writer

"It was when I realized I needed to stop trying to be somebody else and be myself, I actually started to own, accept and love what I had."

—Tracee Ellis Ross, American actress

Think of a person who once made a positive difference in your life. What qualities does that person have that you would like to develop?

What are the most important things in your life right now?
The *big* things.

_____

_____

_____

_____

_____

_____

_____

_____

_____

_____

_____

_____

_____

_____

_____

_____

_____

_____

_____

Describe a time when you were deeply inspired. Be as descriptive as possible.

# Nurture Yourself

There are many lessons that nature teaches us, and it is up to us to take the wisdom and "sow" it into our lives. In farming or gardening, putting in a great deal of work up front lets you reap delicious and beautiful bounty later on down the line. The same goes for any aspect of your life.

List your passions and the ways you can nurture them.

| My Passions | How to Nurture Them |
| --- | --- |
|  |  |
|  |  |
|  |  |
|  |  |
|  |  |
|  |  |
|  |  |

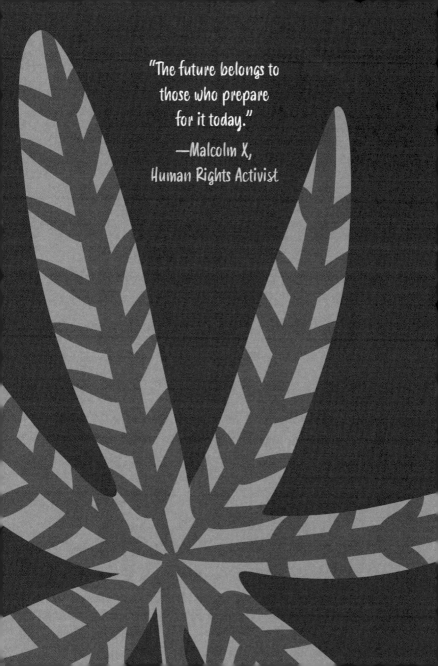

"The future belongs to
those who prepare
for it today."
—Malcolm X,
Human Rights Activist

# Chapter 3

*Make "It" Happen*

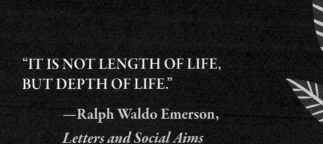

"IT IS NOT LENGTH OF LIFE,
BUT DEPTH OF LIFE."

—Ralph Waldo Emerson,
*Letters and Social Aims*

# Know Your Direction

Habit 3 will help you keep a laser focus on what your dreams are. I often wonder why we find it hard to stay on track for something *so important* to us. It seems almost counterintuitive right? We humans have a talent for getting in our own way, don't we?

Some time ago, a friend of mine named Tiernan was invited to serve as the leader of a group focused on community outreach and service. She had a number of truly important things she was juggling, so she really didn't want to commit to it. She was afraid she couldn't give it her all. But she felt pressured and finally agreed.

> "IF YOU JUST SET OUT TO BE LIKED, YOU WILL BE PREPARED TO COMPROMISE ON ANYTHING AT ANY TIME, AND WOULD ACHIEVE NOTHING."

**—Margaret Thatcher, former prime minister of the United Kingdom**

After being pulled in too many directions (and her stress levels going only one direction: up), she decided to call one of our mutual friends, Éma, to ask if she would serve on the committee instead. Éma listened for a long time to all the wonderful things the group was doing and then said, "Tier, that really does sound like a cool project, a really worthy way to spend my time. Thank you for the invitation. I've gotta pass this time, but I'm super honored."

While Tiernan was constantly under the weather with the overcommitment flu, Éma had built up a tolerance to this sneaky virus by regularly but politely saying "no." Putting first things first is all about learning to prioritize and manage your time so that the most important things in your life are not neglected or shuffled to the sidelines. As Stephen R. Covey so eloquently put it:

> "THE MAIN THING IS TO KEEP THE
> MAIN THING THE MAIN THING."

How can you make *your dreams* happen, when you're too busy making things happen in other areas? Or for other people? As Paulo Coelho wrote in *The Manual of the Warrior of Light*, when you say "yes" to other people, make sure you are not saying "no" to yourself. It's that simple.

Not that you should never be selfless and help someone else out. But if you do it too often, without taking your needs into account, you will end up being pointed and pulled in too many directions. Follow *your* direction. Follow where *your* arrow is pointing.

This chapter is aimed to help you keep track of where you want your life to go, and keeping it that way!

> "WE MUST NOT, IN TRYING TO THINK ABOUT HOW WE
> CAN MAKE A BIG DIFFERENCE, IGNORE THE SMALL DAILY
> DIFFERENCES WE CAN MAKE WHICH, OVER TIME, ADD
> UP TO BIG DIFFERENCES WE OFTEN CANNOT FORESEE."
>
> —**Marian Wright Edelman, American activist**

# Repeat After Me

## AFFIRMATIONS FOR FOLLOWING YOUR ARROW

You should always be your first priority. But if you've forgotten this little piece of advice which helps people keep their sanity, never fear. You can build up this self-love muscle again. Then, and only then, can you focus on your big rocks—your roles in life, or priorities. Starting now.

"LIFE SHRINKS OR EXPANDS IN PROPORTION TO ONE'S COURAGE."

—Anaïs Nin, Cuban American author

"IN THIS LIFE, TO EARN YOUR PLACE YOU HAVE TO FIGHT FOR IT."

—Shakira, Colombian singer

"KNOWING WHAT MUST BE DONE DOES AWAY WITH FEAR."

—Rosa Parks, "Quiet Strength"

I am comfortable saying "no" to others in a kind, firm way, because I know what matters most to me.

I am mindful of where I spend my time.

I make time for those who matter most to me thus strengthening my relationships with others.

I am confident as I am achieving my dream of _____.

Boundaries are healthy—I respect my boundaries and make them clear to others.

I plan my week with a focus on what is Important and Not Urgent.

I let my inner peace radiate to bring others peace.

I work toward making my life balanced. I am positive and peaceful.

My purpose is meaningful and the world needs me to fulfill it.

I do not allow other people's crises and urgencies to dictate my actions.

I spend time daily considering my personal vision, balance, and discipline.

# Finding Your Main Things

## JOURNALING TO STAY ON TRACK

Know what keeps you alive, and own it. We all have our main things and those main things are most often our relationships with those we love. Take ownership of them. Plan time to strengthen and build and maybe even repair those relationships.

"THE MOST DIFFICULT THING IS THE DECISION TO ACT, THE REST IS MERELY TENACITY."

—Amelia Earhart, American pilot

"WHAT YOU DO MAKES A DIFFERENCE, AND YOU HAVE TO DECIDE WHAT KIND OF DIFFERENCE YOU WANT TO MAKE."

—Jane Goodall, British conservationist

"CHANGE YOUR LIFE TODAY. DON'T GAMBLE ON THE FUTURE, ACT NOW, WITHOUT DELAY."

—Simone de Beauvoir, French philosopher

What are my "main things"? What matters most to me?

What are my roles in life? (i.e., teacher, friend, partner, artist, parent.)

What and who would you walk through fire for?

When you were younger, what did you want to change in the world? What do you want to change now?

What are your goals (big rocks a.k.a. priorities) for this week? Organize them in order of priority. Now give them a date. After the week, evaluate how well you did. Did you accomplish everything? What is one thing that you could have done more effectively or efficiently to help you reach your goals?

/ / ———

/ / ———

/ / ———

/ / ———

/ / ———

/ / ———

/ / ———

/ / ———

How much free time do you realistically have per day? List your normal schedule, and highlight the free windows of time. Now reflect—how many more commitments do you think you can really add on? Remember your answer the next time you are asked to commit to something.

6
7
8
9
10
11
12
1
2
3
4
5
6
7
8
9
10

Make a list of responsibilities that you could delegate and the people you can delegate them to or train to be responsible in these areas. Remember, follow your arrow!

Identify and list some things that make you feel stressed out. Now ask yourself why these things make you feel anxious and stressed. How much is in your head? How much is due to overcommitment? How much of what you do could be dropped because it is truly not important? Write and reflect.

_____

_____

_____

_____

_____

_____

_____

_____

_____

_____

_____

_____

_____

_____

_____

_____

_____

_____

What are some ways you like to relax? Think of at least three and then try to do one of these activities per day this week.

What is a commitment that you have not been able to keep this week, month, or year? After you have identified it, make sure you do it by the end of the week.

_____

_____

_____

_____

_____

_____

_____

_____

_____

_____

_____

_____

_____

_____

_____

_____

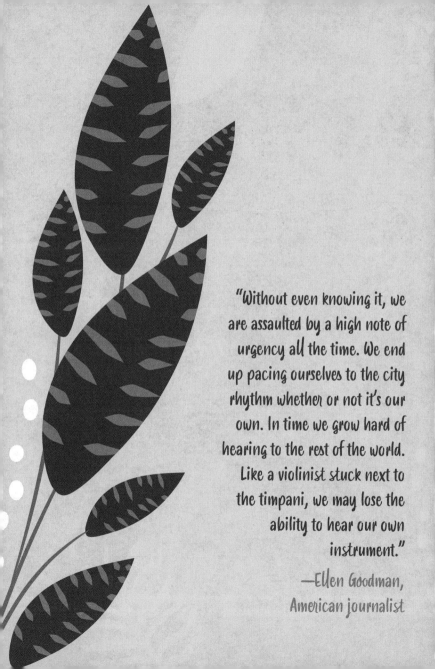

"Without even knowing it, we are assaulted by a high note of urgency all the time. We end up pacing ourselves to the city rhythm whether or not it's our own. In time we grow hard of hearing to the rest of the world. Like a violinist stuck next to the timpani, we may lose the ability to hear our own instrument."

—Ellen Goodman,
American journalist

# Chapter 4

*Think: Abundance*

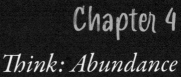

"WHAT YOU BELIEVE TO EXIST IS
WHAT CREATES AND PERSISTS."

—Jaclyn Johnston, American author

# A Wealthy Frame of Mind

Do you want to reach a place where everything (and everyone) works together in harmony? That's what Habit 4 does: it shows the way to mutual benefit and win-win. In nature, everything is connected. Consider the complex interrelationships found in the food chain. Every participant—roaming animals, microorganisms breaking down the dead into fertilizer, light energy from thousands of miles away fueling photosynthesis—fuels life. Anything beyond a casual glance at nature begins to reveal the complex levels of interconnectedness that make it all happen.

> "GREAT CALM, GENEROUS DETACHMENT, SELFLESS LOVE, DISINTERESTED EFFORT: THESE ARE WHAT MAKE FOR SUCCESS IN LIFE. IF YOU CAN FIND PEACE IN YOURSELF AND CAN SPREAD COMFORT AROUND YOU, YOU WILL BE HAPPIER THAN AN EMPRESS."
>
> —Rabindranath Tagore, Bengali poet

This is how our social world works, too. Everyone is valuable, everyone has something to contribute. And most importantly, there is enough success and praise to go around. If one person succeeds, that does not mean we cannot. On the contrary, it means we as a society do, too. We all need to boost one another up, instead of being fearful of others getting ahead of us, being happier than we are, better-looking, more talented, etc.

The problem for many of us comes when we look at our relationships (whether at work or personal) as isolated parts instead of as an organic, highly interrelated whole.

Nature teaches us that businesses, families, and communities are also complex ecosystems, and that what happens in one part affects all parts. It also helps us to realize that every individual is important, and that each of us contribute to the welfare of all.

> "LIFE IS NOT WHAT YOU ALONE MAKE IT. LIFE IS THE INPUT OF EVERYONE WHO TOUCHED YOUR LIFE AND EVERY EXPERIENCE THAT ENTERED IT. WE ARE ALL PART OF ONE ANOTHER."
>
> **—Yuri Kochiyama, Japanese American activist**

Your friend Sophie may have a thriving fitness business, helping tons of women feel their best, but you might have a job as an editor that allows you to publish fun, informative activity books for children. You are still fulfilling your "End in Mind" mission—*enriching other people's lives.*

Think about an area of your life you frequently feel the pull of comparison-thinking; an area of life for which you have a scarcity mindset. Now, let's change your poverty perspective into a wealthy, positive one.

> "EVERYTHING I'VE EVER THOUGHT ABOUT DOING HAS BEEN, IN SOME SENSE, ABOUT HELPING PEOPLE."
>
> **—Jacinda Arden, prime minister of New Zealand**

# Repeat After Me

## AFFIRMATIONS FOR ABUNDANT THOUGHTS

Make fruitfulness part of your every thought. One way to make this happen is by being grateful, even for things that you have not yet received. With an abundant mindset, you find happiness and contentment in the success of others which in turn creates space for good things to come to you.

> "THERE ARE TWO WAYS OF SPREADING LIGHT: TO BE THE CANDLE OR THE MIRROR THAT REFLECTS IT."

—Edith Wharton, *Artemis to Actaeon*

> "THE EFFORT TO IDENTIFY THE ENEMY AS SINGULAR IN FORM IS A REVERSE-DISCOURSE THAT UNCRITICALLY MIMICS THE STRATEGY OF THE OPPRESSOR INSTEAD OF OFFERING A DIFFERENT SET OF TERMS."

—Judith Butler, American philosopher

I have an abundance of talent and insight to offer the world.

I always have more than enough.

I communicate my needs with a balance of courage and consideration.

I seek mutual benefit in all human interactions.

I work to find solutions that benefit all parties.

I am grateful for the blessings that are coming my way.

Wealth is constantly flowing into my life.

I appreciate the uniqueness, inner direction, and proactive nature of others.

I am excited for the new opportunities of others.

I find personal joy and satisfaction when I have an abundance mindset.

As I lift others up, I rise with them. We all rise together.

# Ask Yourself

## JOURNALING FOR A POSITIVITY-RICH MIND

"WHAT DOES IT MATTER HOW MUCH A MAN HAS LAID UP IN HIS SAFE, OR IN HIS WAREHOUSE, HOW LARGE ARE HIS FLOCKS AND HOW FAT HIS DIVIDENDS, IF HE COVETS HIS NEIGHBOR'S PROPERTY, AND RECKONS, NOT HIS PAST GAINS, BUT HIS HOPES OF GAINS TO COME? DO YOU ASK WHAT IS THE PROPER LIMIT TO WEALTH? IT IS, FIRST, TO HAVE WHAT IS NECESSARY, AND, SECOND, TO HAVE WHAT IS ENOUGH."

—Seneca, Roman philosopher

"THE SACRED IS NOT IN HEAVEN OR FAR AWAY. IT IS ALL AROUND US, AND SMALL HUMAN RITUALS CAN CONNECT US TO ITS PRESENCE. AND OF COURSE, THE GREATEST CHALLENGE (AND GIFT) IS TO SEE THE SACRED IN EACH OTHER."

—Alma Luz Villanueva, Mexican American writer

The American poet Gwendolyn Brooks once wrote, "We are each other's harvest: we are each other's business: we are each other's magnitude and bond." What does this mean to you?

_____

_____

_____

_____

_____

_____

_____

_____

_____

_____

_____

_____

_____

_____

_____

_____

_____

_____

Pinpoint an area of your life where you most struggle with comparisons. Acknowledging it is half the battle. How can you develop an abundance mindset here?

_____

_____

_____

_____

_____

_____

_____

_____

_____

_____

_____

_____

_____

_____

_____

_____

_____

_____

Explain why you feel the need to compare, and what you could possibly do to minimize the need to compare yourself.

_____

_____

_____

_____

_____

_____

_____

_____

_____

_____

_____

_____

_____

_____

_____

_____

_____

_____

If you play a sport or compete at work, adopt an everyone-is-awesome attitude. Compliment your opponent no matter who wins. Note how this experience makes you feel.

The next time someone close to you has a life success, be genuinely happy for them and express it. How did it go?

_____

_____

_____

_____

_____

_____

_____

_____

_____

_____

_____

_____

_____

_____

_____

_____

_____

_____

Who has recently helped you accomplish something? Have you thanked them? List them here and determine how you can show your gratitude.

_____

_____

_____

_____

_____

_____

_____

_____

_____

_____

_____

_____

_____

_____

_____

_____

_____

_____

In what area of your life is "scarcity thinking" getting in the way of your happiness? The scarcity mindset causes you to compare, compete, and feel threatened by others.

_____

_____

_____

_____

_____

_____

_____

_____

_____

_____

_____

_____

_____

_____

_____

_____

_____

Think of an upcoming situation in which you anticipate some resistance. What do you want out of this situation and how can you make it work out for everyone?

_____

_____

_____

_____

_____

_____

_____

_____

_____

_____

_____

_____

_____

_____

_____

_____

_____

Think back to a conversation or situation where you "lost" and the other person "won." Reflect on some ways you could have turned it into a mutually beneficial situation.

_____

_____

_____

_____

_____

_____

_____

_____

_____

_____

_____

_____

_____

_____

_____

_____

_____

Describe what you could do to think more abundantly.
Make a conscious effort to celebrate the strengths of yourself
and others, stop comparing, and share resources.

_____

_____

_____

_____

_____

_____

_____

_____

_____

_____

_____

_____

_____

_____

_____

_____

_____

_____

# An Abundant State of Mind

Freewrite here about the things you feel insecure or possessive about, like ensuring you're getting credit for great work or ideas, or even success and promotions. How can you make a conscious effort to reverse your mentality? Remember, abundance breeds abundance.

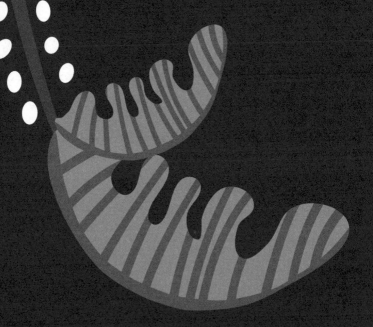

"We are not held back by the love we didn't receive in the past, but by the love we're not extending in the present."
—Marianne Williamson, American author

"You cannot shake hands with a clenched fist."
—Indira Gandhi, Indian activist

# Gratitude Is My Attitude

Every day this week (and the rest of your life, hopefully) write down at least three things you are grateful for.

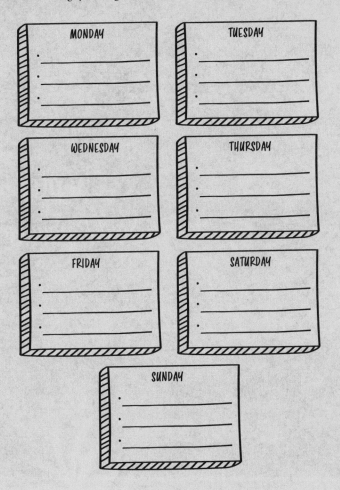

MONDAY
- _____
- _____
- _____

TUESDAY
- _____
- _____
- _____

WEDNESDAY
- _____
- _____
- _____

THURSDAY
- _____
- _____
- _____

FRIDAY
- _____
- _____
- _____

SATURDAY
- _____
- _____
- _____

SUNDAY
- _____
- _____
- _____

# Chapter 5

*Learn Soul Language*

"IF YOU TALK TO A MAN IN A LANGUAGE HE UNDERSTANDS, THAT GOES TO HIS HEAD. IF YOU TALK TO HIM IN *HIS* LANGUAGE, THAT GOES TO HIS HEART."

—Nelson Mandela,
South African activist

# Taking Lessons

• , • •°

Not many people learn another language as fluently as their first, native tongue. There is a reason why. Learning a new language is difficult! You don't just learn new words and conjugations—you learn a whole new way of thinking, and a new rhythm of speaking.

But then one day, you get a real pleasure. Imagine that, after studying it for a little while, you hear it spoken while out and about on the street. Now you suddenly *understand*. You feel like you have a new super power. You might not catch every word the strangers are saying, but you get the gist off the conversation, whereas before it might have just been noise to you. This is the concept that Habit 5 embraces. Listening and speaking in a new way.

> "IF YOU WANT TO BE LISTENED TO, YOU
> SHOULD PUT IN TIME LISTENING."
>
> **—Marge Piercy, American poet and activist**

When I was at my nephew's birthday party at a trampoline theme park (*must* try before you die), watching dozens of kids jumping and performing Olympics-worthy acrobatics, I got into a conversation with the father of one of my nephew's friends. As we got into the subject of his son, he told me, "I can't understand my kid. He just won't listen to me at all."

"Let me restate what you just said," I paused, slightly amused. "You don't understand your son because he won't listen to you?"

"That's right," he replied.

"Let me try again," I said, definitely amused now and trying not to show it. "You don't understand your son because *he* won't listen to *you*?"

"That's what I said!" he impatiently replied.

"I thought that to understand another person, *you* needed to listen to *them*," I suggested.

"Oh..." he said. We sat in silence for a while as the thought sunk in. "Oh!" he said again, and I really believed he almost had it. "Well, I actually do understand him, anyway. I *know* what he's going through. I went through the same things myself." He sat back, satisfied. Never mind.

> WE MUST REMEMBER THAT ONE OF THE MOST INSIDIOUS WAYS OF KEEPING WOMEN AND MINORITIES POWERLESS IS TO LET THEM ONLY TALK ABOUT HARMLESS AND INCONSEQUENTIAL SUBJECTS, OR LET THEM SPEAK FREELY AND NOT LISTEN TO THEM WITH SERIOUS INTENT... TO FINALLY RECOGNIZE OUR OWN INVISIBILITY IS TO FINALLY BE ON THE PATH TOWARD VISIBILITY. INVISIBILITY IS NOT A NATURAL STATE FOR ANYONE."
>
> **—Mitsuye Yamada, Japanese American activist**

I scoffed in my head and watched his son jump wildly with my nephew. This man probably didn't have the vaguest idea of what was really going

on inside his kid's head. He only considered his own perspective and thought he saw the world as it was, including his kid.

That's the case with so many of us. We're filled to the brim with our own expectations, our own autobiography. We want to be understood. Our conversations become soliloquys. Speaking to each other without really paying attention—without ever being *there*—means we never really know what's going on inside another human being.

In order to speak "soul language" sometimes you should opt to just *not* speak. Instead, you need to listen. And, when needed, respond in a way that truly contributes to the conversation in a positive way.

We are all guilty of responding and not listening. But it only takes a few tries to learn (or re-learn) the art of deeply listening. You'll be amazed at how things change for you and others, and how much more meaningful your relationships become.

"In the best conversations, you don't even remember what you talked about, only how it felt. It felt like we were in some place your body can't visit, some place with no ceiling and no walls and no floor and no instruments."

—John Green, American author

# Repeat After Me

## AFFIRMATIONS FOR PEACEFUL COMMUNICATION

Wouldn't it be nice if every interaction with those around us was friendly, clear, and calm? Instead of wishing for it, *actively* seek it. All change starts with you. Allow these affirmations to help you on your way.

"THE MOST IMPORTANT THING IN COMMUNICATION
IS HEARING WHAT ISN'T BEING SAID. THE
ART OF READING BETWEEN THE LINES IS
A LIFE-LONG QUEST OF THE WISE."

—Shannon L. Alder, American author

"LISTENING IS THE BEGINNING OF UNDERSTANDING...
WISDOM IS THE REWARD FOR A LIFETIME OF LISTENING.
LET THE WISE LISTEN AND ADD TO THEIR LEARNING
AND LET THE DISCERNING GET GUIDANCE."

—Proverbs 1:5

I enjoy connecting through ideas and forming bonds with other people.

I express my opinions easily and honestly.

When I listen with my heart and soul, I hear beyond the words people are saying and truly understand them.

I am approachable, have an open mind, and can speak to anybody.

I take a deep breath and center myself in deep understanding of their point of view before replying in stressful conversations.

I listen empathically, I listen for feeling and for meaning.

I excel in my relationships and career because of my strong listening skills.

I actively value others' words, which is why people listen to what I have to say.

I learn so much when I listen without interrupting, and ask questions instead of offering advice.

# Explore Your Conversations

## JOURNAL TO A DEEPER CONNECTION

"WHAT IS FUNDAMENTALLY BEAUTIFUL IS COMPASSION FOR YOURSELF AND FOR THOSE AROUND YOU. THAT KIND OF BEAUTY ENFLAMES THE HEART AND ENCHANTS THE SOUL."

—Lupita Nyong'o, Kenyan-Mexican actress

"[THE BANALITY OF EVIL] IS SIMPLY THE RELUCTANCE EVER TO IMAGINE WHAT THE OTHER PERSON IS EXPERIENCING."

—Hannah Arendt, German American philosopher

"WHEN YOU PUT LOVE OUT IN THE WORLD IT TRAVELS, AND IT CAN TOUCH PEOPLE AND REACH PEOPLE IN WAYS THAT WE NEVER EVEN EXPECTED."

—Laverne Cox, American actress

The next time you have an opportunity to watch people communicate, plug your ears with headphones (or, if you're watching Netflix, just mute) for a few minutes and just watch. What emotions are being communicated that may not come across in words alone?

_____

_____

_____

_____

_____

_____

_____

_____

_____

_____

_____

_____

_____

_____

_____

_____

_____

_____

When in your life have you felt someone really listened to you?
How did this make you feel? How can you make others feel this way?

Think about a relationship you have that you would like to improve. What are some ways you can be a more effective listener and communicator?

When was the last time you had a "great conversation"?
What made this conversation so wonderful?

To the introverts of this world: you're not alone. Starting a conversation can be difficult, whether it be with a stranger or regular acquaintance. What are some unique conversation openers you'd like to try?

It's time to get to know some people better! Below are some questions for you to ask. Make sure to listen without any intent to reply or to tell your own story. It might be fun to write your own answers to these questions here in your journal.

What's the most spontaneous thing you've ever done?

_____

_____

_____

_____

_____

_____

_____

_____

_____

_____

_____

_____

_____

_____

_____

_____

If you had a theme song, what would it be?

_____

_____

_____

_____

_____

_____

_____

_____

What's your hidden talent?

_____

_____

_____

_____

_____

_____

_____

_____

How would a "perfect day" go for you?

_____

_____

_____

_____

_____

_____

_____

_____

If you became Supreme World Ruler, what is the first law you
would make?

_____

_____

_____

_____

_____

_____

_____

_____

If you struggle to be heard, what steps can you take to make sure that your point of view is heard?

_____

_____

_____

_____

_____

_____

_____

_____

_____

_____

_____

_____

_____

_____

_____

_____

_____

_____

# Chapter 6
## *No Root Grows Alone*

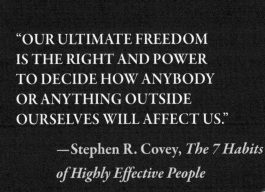

"OUR ULTIMATE FREEDOM
IS THE RIGHT AND POWER
TO DECIDE HOW ANYBODY
OR ANYTHING OUTSIDE
OURSELVES WILL AFFECT US."

—Stephen R. Covey, *The 7 Habits
of Highly Effective People*

# Working Together, Growing Together

• • • •

I was twenty-two when I decided to write for a living. The decision was a sudden one, and went against every instinct inside of me to pursue law or medicine or *anything* but writing. The dream was a tiny secret, and I kept it inside of my mind like a small orchid. But orchids are vines, and soon I found myself inching to tell someone, anyone. I had started writing in my journal each night, but the minute I would sit down to type *anything* I could share to the world, my mind was empty. Shriveling. The orchid was dying.

> "MAYBE WHAT MATTERS IS NOT SO MUCH THE PATH AS WHO WALKS BESIDE YOU."
>
> —**Stacey Lee**, *Under a Painted Sky*

I called my college friends and asked them to meet me in a park nearby. One by one, they agreed, eager to meet after so many summers. Before I could chicken myself out, I decided to start off our meetup with my newfound aspiration. They were quiet, and attentive. I felt like, by telling them, I had finally started to accept the dream myself. Each of my precious friends expressed how happy they were for me, and how they had always envisioned me as a writer. I didn't bother to hold back the sting in my eyes and cried with relief. Suddenly, I could feel the little orchids within them open. Each confessed something profoundly personal, and secret. We talked into the evening, ignoring the mosquitoes sucking the life out of us.

Something happened that afternoon. We became family. Each of our stories became the story of *us*. We felt loved, supported, needed, and valued. This is the soul of Habit 6. Embracing unity and synergy. We are more powerful together.

> "I AM NOT FREE WHILE ANY WOMAN IS UNFREE, EVEN WHEN HER SHACKLES ARE VERY DIFFERENT FROM MY OWN."
>
> **—Audre Lorde, American activist**

Nature teaches us that balance is a dynamic equilibrium. As Dr. Covey wrote,

> When redwood trees mingle their roots, they stand strong against the wind and grow to incredible heights. Birds in a "V" formation can fly nearly twice as far as a lone bird because of the updrafts they create. Two pieces of wood carry exponentially more weight than one piece can bear. We experience synergy every day. One child alone can't reach even one apple; but when another child stands on his shoulders, they can reach all the apples they want. In a conflict situation, synergy can produce an exciting, new-to-the-world solution that makes the conflict irrelevant.

> "FAMILY NOT ONLY NEED CONSIST OF MERELY THOSE WHOM WE SHARE BLOOD, BUT ALSO FOR THOSE WHOM WE'D GIVE BLOOD."
>
> **—Charles Dickens, *Nicholas Nickleby***

When you communicate cooperatively, you open your mind and heart and expressions to new possibilities, new alternatives, and new options. This kind of loving interaction doesn't just happen in friendships. It can also happen in the classroom, for the betterment of everyone. My niece told me this story when I asked her for an example:

> In my physics lab the teacher was demonstrating the principle of momentum and our assignment was to build a catapult, like in medieval times.
>
> It was just me and two guys. We are all very different, so we came up with a ton of different ideas about how to build this bad boy.
>
> One of the guys wanted to use bungee cords to make the launcher flip (he really likes bungee jumping, apparently). *I* wanted to use tension and ropes. Unfortunately, each on their own were literally flops. We really wanted that A, so we put both mechanisms together. The combo gave the pumpkin (we were catapulting pumpkins, by the way) a lot more spring than either would have alone. It was absolutely insane. Our pumpkin literally leapt over the hill and *exploded*. Success! A+ teamwork.

Like my niece and her classmates, consider taking the team effort approach to the challenges you face.

> "BUT PEOPLE NEED LIFT, TOO. PEOPLE DON'T GET MOVING, THEY DON'T SOAR, THEY DON'T ACHIEVE GREAT HEIGHTS, WITHOUT SOMEONE BUOYING THEM UP."
>
> —**Elizabeth Wein,** *Rose Under Fire*

"I can promise you that women working together—linked, informed, and educated—can bring peace and prosperity to this forsaken planet."

—Isabel Allende, Chilean author

# Affirm Your Success

## AFFIRMATIONS FOR CONSCIOUS SYNERGY

Try saying one of these (or all!) aloud each day this week in order to remind you of the power of working together for personal success.

"GROWING APART DOESN'T CHANGE THE FACT THAT FOR A LONG TIME WE GREW SIDE BY SIDE; OUR ROOTS WILL ALWAYS BE TANGLED."

—**Allie Condie,** *Matched*

"IF I WANT MY PEOPLE TO BE FREE, AMERICANS HAVE TO BE FREE."

—**Russell Means, Oglala Lakota activist**

Asking for help is a rally cry for growth.

I reach my goals faster with the support of those around me.

I know that differences in opinions and ideas are a strength, not a weakness.

I embrace and celebrate diversity in people and in thought.

I belong to something bigger than myself.

I become wiser when I solicit feedback.

I become stronger when I am lost and need guidance.

I need others and I know that others need me.

I practice an abundance mindset when I seek third alternatives.

# Explore Your Own Wisdom

## JOURNALING QUESTIONS FOR REFLECTION

Working with a team mindset is not just for the classroom or when fighting for social justice, but for personal success as well. Everyone has something unique to offer, so don't be afraid to approach not only friends, but also colleagues and professors. To get you started, reflect on these questions when facing a particular challenge:

> "WE READ FINE THINGS BUT NEVER FEEL
> THEM TO THE FULL UNTIL WE HAVE GONE
> THE SAME STEPS AS THE AUTHOR."
>
> —John Keats, British poet

> "COLLABORATION IS THE ESSENCE OF LIFE.
> THE WIND, BEES AND FLOWERS WORK
> TOGETHER, TO SPREAD THE POLLEN."
>
> —Amit Ray, Indian author

Who do I know that might have experienced this challenge before? How can I ask for their help?

_____

_____

_____

_____

_____

_____

_____

_____

What is the opportunity in this experience?

_____

_____

_____

_____

_____

_____

_____

_____

When I look back on it, how do I want to remember this experience?

_____

_____

_____

_____

_____

_____

_____

_____

_____

When facing this challenge, am I willing to accept others' points of view
to achieve a "higher" way?

_____

_____

_____

_____

_____

_____

_____

_____

What steps can I take to arrive at synergy?

# Chapter 7

*Make Renewal a Habit*

"AUTUMN.
THE GRACE IN LETTING
DEAD THINGS FALL."

—Darnell Lamont Walker, artist

# A New Reason, a New Season

• •••

Habit 7 is the habit of renewal and self-care—this habit encompasses all the other habits.

> "IN DEALING WITH THOSE WHO ARE UNDERGOING GREAT SUFFERING, IF YOU FEEL 'BURNOUT' SETTING IN, IF YOU FEEL DEMORALIZED AND EXHAUSTED, IT IS BEST, FOR THE SAKE OF EVERYONE, TO WITHDRAW AND RESTORE YOURSELF. THE POINT IS TO HAVE A LONG-TERM PERSPECTIVE."
>
> **—Tenzin Gyatso, 14th Dalai Lama**

How can we find a motive to live the principles of the other habits, to continue on with our goals? In order for a piano to sound good, you must tune it. It doesn't matter how great your technique is, how well you know your scales, if the notes are literally *wrong*. Just like instrumentalists know the importance of having a finely tuned instrument, you must also know how vital it is to take good care of yourself. *You,* after all, *are the instrument!*

> "I ALWAYS GIVE MYSELF SUNDAYS AS A SPIRITUAL BASE OF RENEWAL—A DAY WHEN I DO ABSOLUTELY NOTHING. I SIT IN MY JAMMIES OR TAKE A WALK, AND I ALLOW MYSELF TIME TO BE—CAPITAL B-E—WITH MYSELF."
>
> **—Oprah Winfrey, American television show host**

> Suppose you were to come upon someone in the woods working feverishly to saw down a tree. "What are you doing?" you ask.
>
> "Can't you see?" comes their impatient reply. "I'm sawing down this tree."
>
> "You look exhausted!" you exclaim. "How long have you been at it?"
>
> "Over five hours," they reply, "and I'm beat! This is hard work."
>
> "Well, why don't you take a break for a few minutes and sharpen that saw?" you inquire. "I'm sure it would go a lot faster."
>
> "I don't have time to sharpen the saw," they say emphatically. "I'm too busy sawing."

We sometimes become so fixated on what we're doing, we don't take the time to consider if it's working. The wisdom of the last habit—"Sharpen the Saw"—is to constantly be renewing your mind, your body, your spirit, and your relationships.

Make it a habit to reflect on and acknowledge what you've accomplished so far. To celebrate! You deserve it! Celebration is also *rest*. How can you relax and reminisce if there is chaos? A break never hurt anyone. "Life is short. If you don't stop and look around once in a while, you could miss it." (That's from *Ferris Bueller's Day Off*, which I totally recommend.)

# Repeat After Me

## AFFIRMATIONS FOR YOUR GREATER PURPOSE

Reflect on the following affirmations every day to align to your "center" and regularly press the reset button in your life.

> "SOMETIMES YOU'VE GOT TO LET EVERYTHING GO—PURGE YOURSELF. IF YOU ARE UNHAPPY WITH ANYTHING…WHATEVER IS BRINGING YOU DOWN, GET RID OF IT. BECAUSE YOU'LL FIND THAT WHEN YOU'RE FREE, YOUR TRUE CREATIVITY, YOUR TRUE SELF COMES OUT."

—Tina Turner, American singer

> "IT IS ONLY WHEN WE FEEL DEPRIVED THAT WE RESENT GIVING TO OTHERS. SELF-CARE DOES NOT MEAN YOU STOP CARING ABOUT OTHERS; IT JUST MEANS YOU START CARING MORE ABOUT YOU."

—Beverly Engel, *The Right to Innocence*

I respect my limits and allow periods of rest into my life.

My body is an incredible machine and I treat it with respect.

I surround myself with positive people who help bring out the best in me.

I am attracting new opportunities and wisdom into my life.

I feed my mind with continual learning and education.

I am worthy of love and joy.

I tap into my inner soul in order to find peace and calm.

I am filled with gratitude for the blessings coming my way.

I am fulfilling my greater purpose every day.

I am competent, intelligent, and capable.

# This Is Your Time

• ' • • '

## JOURNALING JUST FOR YOURSELF

"WHEN I'M TIRED, I REST. I SAY, 'I CAN'T
BE A SUPERWOMAN TODAY.' "

—Jada Pinkett Smith, American actress

● ● ●

"LOVE YOURSELF FIRST, AND EVERYTHING ELSE
FALLS IN LINE. YOU REALLY HAVE TO LOVE YOURSELF
TO GET ANYTHING DONE IN THIS WORLD."

—Lucille Ball, American actress

● ● ●

"KNOWING HOW TO BE SOLITARY IS CENTRAL
TO THE ART OF LOVING. WHEN WE CAN BE
ALONE, WE CAN BE WITH OTHERS WITHOUT
USING THEM AS A MEANS OF ESCAPE."

—Bell Hooks, American activist

● ● ●

Make a list of one thing in each of the four dimensions of your life (physical, mental, spiritual, and social/emotional) that is currently *not* working. Maybe you're feeling slightly burned out or uninspired. Explore what feelings you are associating with these areas.

PHYSICAL

MENTAL

SPIRITUAL

SOCIAL/EMOTIONAL

Why do you think these feelings are coming up? How can you make a change?
Reflect and decide on one "next step" for each of the areas you wrote about.

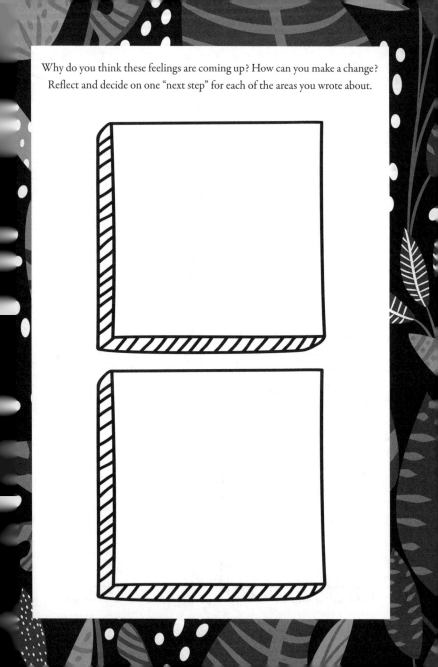

Make a list of activities that you enjoy. Get them all out!
Now, brainstorm how you can sneak in at least one of
these activities every day. Be as creative as possible.

- _____      _____

- _____      _____

                               _____

- _____      _____

                               _____

- _____      _____

                               _____

- _____      _____

                               _____

- _____      _____

                               _____

- _____      _____

                               _____

- _____      _____

                               _____

- _____      _____

                               _____

Write down a new activity that you have been wanting to try, and by the end of the week, try it. After you do, write down what you liked/disliked about it and how you felt about doing something for yourself. Did it feel good?

_____

_____

_____

_____

_____

_____

_____

_____

_____

_____

_____

_____

_____

_____

_____

_____

_____

_____

What does "loving yourself" mean to you?

_____
_____
_____
_____
_____
_____
_____
_____
_____
_____
_____
_____
_____
_____
_____
_____
_____
_____
_____
_____
_____

What are your favorite downtime activities? How do *you* relax?

_____

_____

_____

_____

_____

_____

_____

_____

_____

_____

_____

_____

_____

_____

_____

_____

_____

_____

_____

Think about the times you've felt spiritually refreshed.
What were you doing? Who were you with?

_____

_____

_____

_____

_____

_____

_____

_____

_____

_____

_____

_____

_____

_____

_____

_____

_____

_____

What is one mental goal that you have set for yourself? Write it down, and make sure it's clear. Now, what is one thing you can do today to make progress on that goal? Give your goal a deadline.

_____

_____

_____

_____

_____

_____

_____

_____

_____

_____

_____

_____

_____

_____

_____

_____

_____

_____

What is the "reason" you are living for now? In other words, what greater purpose drives you?

_____

_____

_____

_____

_____

_____

_____

_____

_____

_____

_____

_____

_____

_____

_____

_____

_____

_____

_____

Do you begin the week mentally refreshed? List some ways
you can start the week off feeling calm and focused.

_____

_____

_____

_____

_____

_____

_____

_____

_____

_____

_____

_____

_____

_____

_____

_____

_____

_____

Are you spending time each day renewing your body, mind, heart, and spirit? Write your own routine for daily renewal. Where can you improve?

_____

_____

_____

_____

_____

_____

_____

_____

_____

_____

_____

_____

_____

_____

_____

_____

_____

_____

"Learning to love yourself is like learning to walk—essential, life-changing, and the only way to stand tall."

—Vironika Tugaleva, Ukrainian author

"You have to believe in yourself. You have to take care of yourself, work for yourself, believe in yourself, and also be patient with yourself. Learn when not to push too hard, and give yourself a break."

—Salma Hayek, Mexican American actress

# Conclusion

## *Affirm Your Life Now*

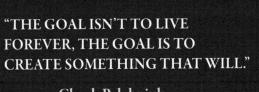

"THE GOAL ISN'T TO LIVE
FOREVER, THE GOAL IS TO
CREATE SOMETHING THAT WILL."

—Chuck Palahniuk

# Visualize Your Dreams

Whether you're the owner of a yoga studio, a cook, writer, stay-at-home mom, store clerk, community college student, or CEO, your life can be fulfilling if you give it the deepest effort and care you have within you. You will not always be spared difficulties or challenges—but you *will* experience a deep sense of purpose as you share the best of your talents, the strongest of your passions, and the commitment of your conscience.

"NEVER LIMIT YOURSELF BECAUSE OF OTHERS'
LIMITED IMAGINATION; NEVER LIMIT OTHERS
BECAUSE OF YOUR OWN LIMITED IMAGINATION."

—Mae Jemison, engineer and former NASA astronaut

How do you envision your most fruitful, effective life?

_____
_____
_____
_____
_____
_____
_____
_____
_____
_____
_____
_____
_____
_____
_____
_____
_____
_____
_____
_____
_____

We have covered deep topics through this journal, each of which will contribute to your fulfillment and life effectiveness. As you know by now, "effectiveness" brings the maximum long-term beneficial results possible. Tapping into your human gift of self-awareness over and over again continuously renews your commitment to improvement. This commitment empowers you to move on an upward spiral of growth and continuous improvement.

To keep progressing we must learn, commit, and do. Learn, commit, and do. *Learn, commit and do*. Again, and again, and again.

You will not be able to accomplish your purpose if you don't keep renewing the habits of effectiveness. You cannot appreciate how far you have come, and how much you have, if you don't take a look around and express sincere gratitude.

And you certainly can't have happy, meaningful relationships without having a healthy one with yourself first—*the private victory precedes the public victory*—achieving your dreams comes from living from the inside-out.

What does "effectiveness" look like to you?

# Create Your Own Affirmations

The inspiration and affirmations in this book are intended to provide the first step toward your personal betterment. Once you become comfortable, *you* can be your own guide. As you build your confidence and focus, you may learn great lessons that you wish to share with the world. Please do! You may also wish to create your own affirmations for your life.

If you would like to start now, affirmations usually require five basic ingredients. They should be:

Personal
Positive
Visual
Set in the present tense
Emotional

Here is a sample affirmation:

It is deeply satisfying that I respond with wisdom, confidence, and self-control when a crisis comes up at work.

Emotional / Personal / Visual / Present Tense / Positive

This affirmation sample captures a desire you might wish to manifest. Instead of focusing on, "I always get frustrated when there's a problem at work," you have now transformed your mindset. You now have a *solution*, when before you just had a problem. When you envision it, and make it part of your everyday consciousness, you will be surprised by how much easier it is to achieve.

*The hardest work is in the mind.*

Try crafting a few affirmations today to close out this journey we've been on. You can write them down in the following section. Don't worry about doing it "correctly." As long as it works for *you*...it works.

# Affirm Your Life

• ، • •

## AFFIRMATIONS FOR ME—LOVE, ME

# Sources

Covey, Sean, *The 7 Habits of Highly Effective Teens*, Simon & Schuster, 1998, 2014.

Covey, Stephen R., *The 7 Habits of Highly Effective People*, Simon & Schuster, 1989, 2004, 2020.

Covey, Stephen R. *The Nature of Leadership*, FranklinCovey Co. (1998).

Clarridge, Christine. "Remembering Rosa Parks: Words of wisdom from 'mother of the civil rights movement,'" December 1, 2016. https://www.seattletimes.com/life/remembering-rosa-parks-words-of-wisdom-from-mother-of-civil-rights/

Edgar Johnson, "*A Christmas Carol* Criticizes England's Economic System," *Readings on Charles Dickens*, ed. Clarice Swisher, Greenhaven Press, 1998, 86–93.

Nivedita Mehta, *CalmerSutra: Be Calm, Confident & Happy!* Hay House India, 2014.

# About the Author

## BECCA ANDERSON

Becca Anderson comes from a long line of teachers and preachers from Ohio and Kentucky. The teacher side of her family led her to become a woman's studies scholar and the author of the bestselling *The Book of Awesome Women*. An avid collector of affirmations, meditations, prayers and blessings, she helps run a "Gratitude and Grace Circle" that meets monthly at homes, churches, and bookstores in the San Francisco Bay Area where she currently resides.

Becca Anderson credits her spiritual practice and daily prayer with helping her recover from cancer and wants to share this encouragement with anyone who is facing difficulty in life with *Prayers for Hard Times* and her latest, *The Woman's Book of Prayer*. The author of *Think Happy to Stay Happy* and *Every Day Thankful*, Becca Anderson shares prayers and affirmations, inspirational writings and suggested acts of kindness at thedailyinspoblog.wordpress.com. She also blogs about awesome women at theblogofawesomewomen.wordpress.com. Find her at @AndersonBecca_ on Twitter, @BeccaAndersonWriter on Facebook, and @BeccaAndersonWriter on Instagram.

# INSPIRED BY STEPHEN R. COVEY

Dr. Stephen R. Covey passed away in 2012 leaving behind an unmatched legacy of teachings about leadership, time management, effectiveness, success, and love and family. A multimillion-copy bestselling author of self-help and business classics, Dr. Covey strove to help readers recognize the principles that would lead them to personal and professional effectiveness. His seminal work, *The 7 Habits of Highly Effective People*, transformed the way people think and act upon their problems with a compelling, logical, and well-defined process.

As an internationally respected leadership authority, family expert, teacher, organizational consultant, and author, his advice gives insight to millions. He sold more than 30 million books (in 50 languages), and *The 7 Habits of Highly Effective People* was named the #1 Most Influential Business Book of the Twentieth Century. He was the author of *The 3rd Alternative, The 8th Habit, The Leader in Me, First Things First*, and many other titles. He held an MBA from Harvard and a doctorate from Brigham Young University. He lived with his wife and family in Utah.

# Also by Becca Anderson

*The Book of Awesome Women Writers: Medieval Mystics, Pioneering Poets, Fierce Feminists and First Ladies of Literature*

*Let Me Count the Ways: Wise and Witty Women on the Subject of Love*

*Friendship Isn't a Big Thing, It's a Million Little Things: The Art of Female Friendship*

*The Woman's Book of Prayer: 365 Blessings, Poems and Meditations*

*Prayers for Calm: Meditations, Affirmations and Prayers to Soothe Your Soul*

*Badass Affirmations: The Wit and Wisdom of Wild Women*

*Badass Women Give the Best Advice: Everything You Need to Know About Life and Love*

*Think Happy to Stay Happy: The Awesome Power of Learned Optimism*

*Real Life Mindfulness: Meditations for a Calm and Quiet Mind*

*The Book of Awesome Women: Boundary Breakers, Freedom Fighters, Sheroes and Female Firsts*

*Prayers for Hard Times: Reflections, Meditations and Inspirations for Hope and Comfort*

*Everyday Thankful: Blessings, Graces and Gratitudes*

Mango Publishing, established in 2014, publishes an eclectic list of books by diverse authors—both new and established voices—on topics ranging from business, personal growth, women's empowerment, LGBTQ studies, health, and spirituality to history, popular culture, time management, decluttering, lifestyle, mental wellness, aging, and sustainable living. We were recently named 2019 *and* 2020's #1 fastest growing independent publisher by *Publishers Weekly*. Our success is driven by our main goal, which is to publish high quality books that will entertain readers as well as make a positive difference in their lives.

Our readers are our most important resource; we value your input, suggestions, and ideas. We'd love to hear from you—after all, we are publishing books for you!

Please stay in touch with us and follow us at:

Facebook: Mango Publishing
Twitter: @MangoPublishing
Instagram: @MangoPublishing
LinkedIn: Mango Publishing
Pinterest: Mango Publishing

Sign up for our newsletter at www.mangopublishinggroup.com and receive a free book!

Join us on Mango's journey to reinvent publishing, one book at a time.